A Reader's Guide

A Reading List
and Plan for
Classical Students
and Parents

A Reader's Guide
© Classical Academic Press, 2004
Version 2.6

A special publication produced in conjunction with
Covenant Christian Academy, Harrisburg PA.

www.CovenantChristianAcademy.us

All rights reserved. This publication may not be reproduced, stored in a retrieval system or transmitted, in any form or by any means, without the prior permission in writing of Classical Academic Press.

Classical Academic Press
3920 Market Street
Camp Hill, PA 17011

www.ClassicalAcademicPress.com

Book design & cover by:
Rob Baddorf

A Reader's Guide

*A Reading List and Plan for
Classical Students and Parents*

Preface
By Christopher Perrin and Leslie Rayner

After six years of research, review, reading and collaborating, the Curriculum Committee of Covenant Christian Academy (CCA) has produced a Reading List and Guide for CCA students and parents. Leslie Rayner, the Committee Co-Chair is responsible for compiling this list with input and review from the rest of the committee. This document has been designed with three basic goals and five specific objectives. We thought it would be helpful to list them for you at the outset:

Goals
1. Encourage and foster a life-long love of reading
2. Develop in students a taste for the best literature
3. Guide the reading activity of students in an incremental, topical fashion

Objectives

1. Give students guidance and direction as they choose books for independent reading and book reports (as required by CCA in various grades).

2. Help students, teachers and parents make intelligent, wise decisions regarding what books students read, enabling them to select books at the right reading level, in the right genre and of appropriate topic and content.

3. Insure that parents read more good literature themselves and with their children (e.g., reading aloud to children, discussing books that both parent and child read).

4. Provide students with a record of the books they read in order to grant them the satisfaction of seeing their reading achievements and to motivate them to read more great books.

5. Provide parents and teachers with a record of the books that students read in order to help parents and teachers guide reading, suggest new books and avenues of study, cultivate interests and build new areas of interest.

At Covenant Christian Academy, our desire is not only for students to learn how to read, but also to acquire a passion for reading. We aim to cultivate a life-long love of reading excellent books that span generations and are worth reading over again. The list of books in the *CCA Reading Guide* has been compiled to encourage reading what CCA considers superb literature while allowing for individual choice and preference. We hope that parents and children will come to know and love some of the best authors and literature that exist, and develop a lifelong love of reading!

God is a Being who speaks, who has fashioned creatures who speak. Christ himself is called the "Word." He has also chosen to preserve a written record (the Scripture) of his saving acts for our salvation, edification and instruction. The Bible itself is full of many kinds of literature--history, narration, poetry, philosophy, parables, letters. Christians have been called from ancient times "people of the Book;" consequently Christians have always been interested in books, in reading them and writing them. As speaking beings and as Christians, we wish to pass on this love of Scripture and literature to our children.

If we are going to pass on literature to our children, why not give them the best we have found? And why not give it to them as intelligently as we can, guiding their reading according to their ability, interest and maturity? We have tried to do this in our guide, so that CCA parents can benefit from the labor of our committee and staff who have put their heads together towards this end. Why another guide when there are others to consult? Indeed we have consulted many reading guides. While they have been very helpful, we have frequently found that these guides vary in scope and disagree with one another, compelling us to do a great deal of our own reading and assessment. Additionally, we have tried to cull books that fit well with our curriculum, philosophy and students here at CCA, which no other guide could do. It is also integrated with the historical periods that our children study. This guide, therefore, is tailor-made for classically-educated, Christian students, in a fairly academic school. We believe, however, that other families, students and schools will benefit from this guide as well.

So let the children read. Let the grown-up children read. An education--with hard work, adventure, surprise and change--awaits us all. We imagine and pray for many wonderful hours in which we are transported by great words from great minds--words so well chosen that they "awaken sensibility, great emotions, and understanding of truth."[1]

Ensconced with great books, our children will travel to places which we cannot take them, to times we cannot go. Lives will be lived, loves lost and gained, battles fought and won. Virtue can be taught and stoked; empathy, understanding, conviction, courage and compassion can all find strength and depth. As our children travel the world among the pages, we will find them not just entertained but one day made wise. The right book at the right time can change the course of a child's life; the right story, the right biography can awaken an interest or calling that may serve the church and culture as much as it surprises mom and dad. Since you will be reading with your children, you will likely find that something in you wakes up too.

Because a child's understanding and character can be shaped and influenced by what he reads, "it is imperative that their books be of high caliber."[2] The books listed in the *CCA Reading Guide* have been carefully selected. These books have been examined to insure that they are excellent examples of English writing containing proper grammar and syntax, skillful language of various styles, vivid description and gripping narration and dialogue. Many of

---
[1] Hunt, Gladys, *Honey for a Child's Heart,* Grand Rapids, MI, Zondervan, 1989, p. 14.
[2] *Ibid.*, p. 12

the books also contain appealing visual illustrations. The content of these books has also been scrutinized, to insure that the themes are age-appropriate. We have searched for books that are generally wholesome and affirming to a Christian worldview, even when they may portray the realities of this world's brokenness and sin. We have avoided books with little or no redemptive value, and books that contain patently offensive or sacrilegious language. We have used these criteria for the selection of both classics and more recent publications. Some of the books selected for older students (e.g., grades 10-12) will require critical, Christian analysis as the themes will be more complex and mature.

The following information gleaned from *The Book Tree* is an overview of our literary objectives for each stage of CCA's Grammar, Dialectic, and Rhetoric schools.

Grammar Students

Beginning readers should be given character-building stories along with those that celebrate the joys of childhood. The plots should reward the good and punish the wicked, and never condone or gloss over sinful behaviors. Authoritative figures (parents, teachers, pastors, etc.) may have flaws, but should be generally virtuous and depicted in a positive light. Children in this stage love animal adventure stories, mythology, Arthurian legends, fables, and tales of heroes (including those of our faith and American heritage).

Dialectic Students

Students at this stage need to read books for reports and

research as well as for pleasure, and should be voracious readers by now. It is imperative to introduce dialectic students to a variety of excellent books that insure the development of a good literary taste. Their creative imaginations should be cultivated with well-written fantasies, thrillers, mysteries, science fiction, and narratives about growing up and coming of age. They should also be regularly reading biographies and historical fiction.

Rhetoric Students

Tastes in this stage become more precise and refined. Once students find their reading niche, they should be directed to more excellent books within that niche, though not exclusively. Rhetoric students should be encouraged to read the best classic novels, plays, and poems. Students tend to relish these works earlier than we think. Reading these books will aid them in developing a "sharp intellect, an analytical mind, and a well-tuned sense of humor"[3] and provide them with vocabulary, figures of speech and writing style that they can emulate in their own writing and speaking.

Augustine heard children next door singing a Latin song that featured the refrain "Tolle et lege" (take up and read). When he heard that he was moved to take up the Bible and read. His hand fell to the book of Romans and his life began its change of direction, that makes him a familiar name today. Who knows what awaits as our children take up Scripture and great books and begin to read?

---

[3] *Ibid.*, p. 14.

While we hope the list that follows is helpful, it is an evolving list. We will update this list regularly with additional titles that have escaped our attention or that are recommended to us. You may use the provided lines at the end of each section for adding new titles. At the end of the Reading Guide is a section of extra pages for recording additional titles you have read or hope to read thus allowing this Reading Guide to be a life long journal. Please send suggested titles for our reading list to office@covenantchristianacademy.net.

CCA History Timeline Key

To understand our placement of historical fiction titles, we have included the following history timeline.

Grade	Historical Period
1st	Local Pennsylvania History
2nd	Ancient Egypt
3rd	Ancient Greece and Rome
4th	Middle Ages, Renaissance and Reformation
5th	American History: Explorers to 1815
6th	American History: 1815 to the Present
7th	Ancient Civilizations (Mesopotamia, China, Egypt, India)
8th	Classical Greece and Rome
9th	Middle Ages to the Renaissance
10th	Early Modern Europe
11th	American History
12th	Modern World History

Resources

1. Bloom, Jan, *Who Should We Then Read? Authors of Good Books for Children and Young Adults*, Cokato, MN, BooksBloom, 2001
2. Elizabeth McCallum and Jane Scott, *The Book Tree: A Christian Reference for Children's Literature*, Moscow, ID, Canon Press, 2001
3. Hatcher, Carolyn, *Let the Authors Speak: A Guide to Worthy Books Based on Historical Setting*, Joelton, TN, Old Pinnacle Publishing, 1994
4. Hunt, Gladys, *Honey For a Child's Heart: The Imaginative Use of Books in Family Life*, Grand Rapids, MI, Zondervan, 1989
5. *Tall Oaks Classical School Literature List*, Tall Oaks Classical School, 2000-2001
6. Wilson, Elizabeth, *Books Children Love: A Guide to the Best Children's Literature*, Wheaton, IL, Crossway Books, 1987

Covenant Christian Academy
Recommended Literature List

CCA grades are grouped into:
Kindergarten, Lower Grammar (1ˢᵗ - 3ʳᵈ), Upper Grammar (4ᵗʰ - 6ᵗʰ), Dialectic (7ᵗʰ - 9ᵗʰ), and Rhetoric (10ᵗʰ - 12ᵗʰ).

Level: The approximate level of difficulty is rated for each title within each grade grouping.

1	easy
2	average
3	challenging

Notations:

M	mandatory title read in a particular grade
TRA	teacher reads aloud to class
I	title read independently, related to particular grade historically

Genre:

F	fiction
NF	non-fiction

P	poetry
HF	historical fiction (realistic fiction set in particular time period)
H	historical (historical accounts)
D	drama
B	biography
AB	autobiography
RF	realistic fiction (contains characters and situations that could happen)
SF	science fiction (contains gadgets, inventions, or imaginary worlds)
Fa	fantasy/fables/fairy tales/myths/legends (characters enter other worlds or are not human)
Ad	adventure (unlikely, exciting and/or surprising stories)
M	mystery

Kindergarten Literature List

These titles are generally used as teacher read-alouds during the first three quarters of the school year. Many students may begin reading some of these with teacher guidance or independently by the fourth quarter.

Title	Author
Little Fur Family, The	Brown
Gingerbread Boy, The	Galdone
Little Red Hen, The	Galdone
Three Bears and Goldilocks, The	Galdone
Three Billy Goats Gruff, The	Galdone
Three Little Pigs, The	Galdone
Bread and Jam for Francis	Hoban
Danny and the Dinosaur	Hoff
Biggest House in the World (and others by author)	Lionni
Inch by Inch	Lionni
Wait and See	Muench
Little Engine That Could, The	Piper
Curious George (and others in series)	Rey
Relatives Came, The	Rylant
Cat in the Hat	Seuss
Cat in the Hat Comes Back	Seuss
Hop on Pop	Seuss
Green Eggs and Ham	Seuss
Gregory the Terrible Eater	Sharmat
Caps for Sale	Slobodkin
Red is Best	Stinson

Additional Titles

Title	Author	Date read
notes:		
notes:		
notes:		
notes:		
notes:		
notes:		
notes:		
notes:		
notes:		
notes:		
notes:		

Lower Grammar School List
(1ˢᵗ - 3ʳᵈ)

Title	Author	Genre	Notations	Level	√
Aesop's Fables for Children (selections)	Aesop	Fa	M-3 TRA	3	
Corn is Maize	Aliki	F	TRA-1	1	
Story of William Penn, The	Aliki	B/H	TRA-1	1	
Miss Nelson is Missing	Allard	F	TRA-2	2	
Miss Nelson (+ sequels)	Allard	F		2	
An Amish Year	Ammon	HF	TRA-1	2	
Amish Horses	Ammon	HF	TRA-1	2	
Billy and Blaze	Anderson	Ad	TRA-2	2	
Blaze (sequels)	Anderson	Ad		2	
Emperor's New Clothes, The	Anderson	Fa		2	
Anderson's Fairy Tales (selections)	Anderson	Fa	M-3 TRA	3	
Ugly Duckling, The	Anderson	Fa		3	
History Detectives, Ancient Egypt	Ardagh	HF	I-2	1	
Mr. Popper's Penguins	Atwater	Fa		2	
Folks in the Valley	Aylesworth	HF	TRA-1	2	
Adventures in Ancient Egypt	Bailey	HF	I-2	1	
Big Book of Brambly Hedge, The	Barklem	Fa		2	
Little Rabbit (+ any in series)	Bate	F		1	
Madeline (+ any in series)	Bemelman	RF		1	
George, the Drummer Boy	Benchley	HF		1	
Sam, the Minute Man	Benchley	HF		1	
Amish Home	Bial	HF	TRA-1	2	

Lower Grammar

Title	Author	Genre	Notations	Level	√
Bear Called Paddington, A	Bond	Fa		2	
Boy Who Loved to Draw, The	Brenner	B/H	TRA-1	2	
Hat, The	Brett	F		1	
Milly, Molly, Mandy Storybook	Brisley	RF		3	
Stone Soup	Brown	Fa		1	
Dick Whittington and His Cat	Brown	Fa		2	
Daniel's Duck	Bulla	F		2	
Little Pilgrim's Progress	Bunyan/ Taylor	Fa	M-3	3	
Adventures of Old Mr. Toad	Burgess	F		2	
Little House	Burton	F	M-1	1	
Mike Mulligan and the Steam Shovel	Burton	F		1	
Katy & the Big Snow	Burton	F		1	
Pancakes, Pancakes!	Carle	RF		1	
Alice in Wonderland	Carroll	Fa		3	
Chanticlear and the Fox	Chaucer/ Cooney	Fa	TRA-1	1	
Henry Huggins	Cleary	RF	M-2	2	
Ribsey	Cleary	RF		2	
Henry Huggins sequels	Cleary	F		2	
Ralph S. Mouse	Cleary	Fa		3	
Ramona Quimby, Age 8	Cleary	RF		3	
Runaway Ralph	Cleary	Fa		3	
King's Giraffe, The	Collier	F		2	
Pinocchio of C. Collodi	Collodi	Fa		3	
Children's Homer, The	Colum	Fa	M-3 TRA	3	

Lower Grammar

Title	Author	Genre	Notations	Level	√
Golden Fleece, The	Colum	Fa/H	I-3	3	
Racso and the Rats of NIMH (sequel to Mrs. Frisby....)	Conly	Fa		3	
Ancient Greece of Odysseus	Connolly	HF	I-3	2	
Cavalryman, The	Connolly	HF	I-3	1	
Legionary, The	Connolly	HF	I-3	1	
Miss Rumphius	Cooney	F	TRA-1	1	
Against the World: The Odyssey of Athanasius	Coray	HF	I-3	3	
Little Lame Prince, The	Craik	Fa		3	
Book of Greek Myths (selections)	D'Aulaire	Fa/H	I-3	3	
Charlie and the Chocolate Factory	Dahl	Fa		3	
Bears on Hemlock Mountain, The	Dalgliesh	F	M-2	2	
Courage of Sarah Noble, The	Dalgliesh	H	M-2	2	
Thanksgiving Story, The	Dalgliesh	H		2	
Henner's Lydia	Dalgliesh	HF	TRA-1	3	
Andy and the Lion	Daugherty	F		2	
Tales From the Arabian Nights	Dawood (retold by)	Fa		3	
Thee, Hannah	DeAngeli	HF		3	
Along Came a Dog	DeJong	F		3	
Wheel on the School, The	DeJong	RF	M-3	3	
Children's Classic Poetry	Derrydale Books	P		2	
Tut's Mummy	Donnelly	NF	M-2	2	
Moonwalk: First Trip to the Moon	Donnelly	NF		2	
Mystery of the Hieroglyphs	Donoughue	H	I-2	1	

Lower Grammar

Title	Author	Genre	Notations	Level	√
Black Stallion	Farley	RF		3	
Drummer Hoff	Emberly	F		1	
Moses	Fisher	B	I-2	1	
Theseus & the Minotaur	Fisher	Fa	I-3	1	
Story About Ping, The	Flack/ Wiese	Fa		1	
Where Time Stands Still	Foster	HF	TRA-1	2	
House That Jack Built	Fransconi	F		2	
Corduroy	Freeman	Fa	M-1	1	
George Washington's Breakfast	Fritz	F		2	
George Washington's Mother	Fritz	H		2	
Cabin Faced West, The	Fritz	H	TRA-1	2	
Just a Few Words, Mr. Lincoln	Fritz	H	TRA-1	2	
Can't you Make Them Behave, King George?	Fritz	H		2	
Stopping By the Woods on a Snowy Evening	Frost (Scholastic)	P		1	
Reuben & the Quilt	Good	HF	TRA-1	2	
Reuben & the Blizzard	Good	HF	TRA-1	2	
Little Toot	Gramatky	Fa		1	
Alexander the Great	Green	B	I-3	2	
Grimm's Fairy Tales (selections)	Grimm	Fa	M-3 TRA	3	
Big Snow, The	Hader	F		1	
Oxcart Man	Hall	RF	TRA-1	1	
Three Young Pilgrims	Harness	HF		2	
Goose That Was A Watchdog, The	Hays	RH		2	
First Thanksgiving, The	Hayward	HF		1	

PAGE 16

Lower Grammar

Title	Author	Genre	Notations	Level	√
Reason for a Flower	Heller	NF		2	
Misty of Chincoteague (+ sequels)	Henry	RF		3	
Brighty of the Grand Canyon	Henry	RF		3	
Bedtime for Francis (+ any in series)	Hoban	F		1	
Bread and Jam for Francis	Hoban	F		1	
St. George and the Dragon	Hodges	Fa		2	
Sammy the Seal	Hoff	Fa		1	
Great Wonder, The	Howard	H	I-2	1	
Tale of Three Trees, The	Hunt	Fa		1	
Gift for Grandpa, A	Hunt	RF		2	
Trail of Apple Blossoms	Hunt	HF		3	
Joel, A Boy of Galilee	Johnston	RF	M-3 TRA	3	
Phantom Toll Booth, The	Juster	Fa		3	
Snowy Day, The	Keats	F		1	
Paul Bunyan	Kellogg	Fa		1	
People Apart	Kenna	HF	TRA-1	2	
Just-So Stories	Kipling	Fa		3	
Seventh and Walnut	Knight	H	TRA-1	3	
Farm, The	Knight	RF	TRA-1	3	
Winter at Valley Forge, The	Knight	H	TRA-1	3	
Conqueror and Hero: The Search for Alexander	Krensky	H		3	
Egypt	Krensky	H	I-2	1	
Pompeii…Buried Alive!	Kunhardt	H	I-3	1	
Red Balloon	LaMarisse	RF	TRA-1	1	
Tales From Shakespeare	Lamb	P		3	
Arabian Nights	Lang (edited)	Fa		3	

Lower Grammar

Title	Author	Genre	Notations	Level	√
Boy Who Loved Music (Haydn)	Lasker	B		3	
Sugaring Time	Lasky	RF		2	
Jem's Island	Lasky	RF		2	
Librarian Who Measured the Earth	Lasky	B	I-3	1	
Rabbit Hill	Lawson	Fa		3	
Ben and Me	Lawson	Fa/H	TRA-1	3	
Ferdinand	Leaf	Fa		1	
Floss series	Lewis	F		2	
Frederick (+ any in series)	Lionni	Fa		1	
Swimmy	Lionni	Fa		1	
Trojan Horse, The	Little	H	I-3	1	
Magic Fish, The	Littledale	Fa		1	
Frog and Toad Are Friends	Lobel	Fa	M-1	1	
Frog and Toad Together (+ any in series)	Lobel	Fa		1	
Mouse Soup	Lobel	Fa		1	
Fables	Lobel	Fa		3	
Owl at Home	Lobel	Fa		1	
5000 Year Old Puzzle	Logan	HF	I-2	1	
Senefer	Lumpkin	B	I-2	1	
Mrs. Pigglewiggle	MacDonald	Fa	TRA-2	2	
Caleb's Story	Maclachlan	RF		1	
Sarah, Plain and Tall	MacLachlan	RF		3	
All the Places to Love	MacLachlan	RF		2	
Great Pyramid, The	Mann	H	I-2	1	
Blueberries for Sal	McCloskey	RF		1	
Make Way for Ducklings	McCloskey	Fa		1	

Lower Grammar

Title	Author	Genre	Notations	Level	√
Homer Price	McCloskey	RF		3	
One Morning in Maine	McCloskey	RF		2	
Lentil	McCloskey	RF		2	
Time of Wonder	McCloskey	RF		2	
Mouton's Impossible Dream	McGrory	Fa	TRA-1	1	
Winnie the Pooh	Milne	Fa	M-2 TRA	2	
World of Christopher Robin, The	Milne	Fa		2	
House at Pooh Corner	Milne	Fa		2	
Hieroglyphs	Milton	H	I-2	1	
Little Bear	Minarik	Fa	M-1	1	
Little Bear's Visit (+ any in series)	Minarik	Fa		1	
Tomahawks and Trombones	Mitchell	H	TRA-1	2	
Down Buttermilk Lane	Mitchell	HF	TRA-1	2	
One Bad Thing About Father, The	Monjo	B		2	
Reuben & the Fire	Moss	HF	TRA-1	1	
Ancient Greece	Nicholson	H	I-3	1	
Mrs. Frisby and the Rats of NIMH	O'Brien	Fa		3	
Amelia Bedelia	Parish	F	M-2	2	
Kermit the Hermit	Peet	Fa		2	
True Story of Pocahontas	Penner	B		1	
Song of the Swallows	Politi	P		2	
Peter Rabbit (selections from)	Potter	Fa	M-2	2	
Stories of the Pilgrims	Pumprey	H		3	

Lower Grammar

Title	Author	Genre	Notations	Level	√
Wonder Clock, The	Pyle	Fa		3	
Cecily G. & the Monkeys	Rey	Fa		2	
Curious George (+ any in series)	Rey	Fa		1	
Keep the Lights Burning, Abbie	Roup	H		1	
Classic Myths to Read Aloud	Russell	Fa	M-3 TRA	3	
Henry and Mudge series	Rylant	Fa		1	
Thimbleberry Stories	Rylant	Fa		2	
When I Was Young in the Mountains	Rylant	RF		1	
Tutankhamen's Gift	Sabuda	HF	I-2	1	
Pioneer Bear	Sandin	RF		1	
Young Ben Franklin	Santrey	B/H	TRA-1	3	
Chester Cricket's New Home	Selden	Fa		3	
Cricket in Times Square	Selden	Fa		3	
Where the Wild Things Are	Sendak	Fa		1	
I Can Lick 30 Tigers Today	Seuss	Fa		1	
One Fish, Two Fish	Seuss	Fa		1	
There's a Wocket in My Pocket	Seuss	Fa		1	
Nate the Great (+ sequels)	Sharmat	Fa		2	
Rescuers, The	Sharp	Fa		3	
Miss Bianca	Sharp	Fa		3	
Encyclopedia Brown (+ any in series but not for book reports)	Sobol	RF		2	
Bronze Bow, The	Speare	HF	M-3	3	
Little Sure Shot: Story of Annie Oakley	Spinner	B		2	

PAGE 20

Lower Grammar

Title	Author	Genre	Notations	Level	√
King Without a Shadow, The	Sproul	RF		3	
Priest with the Dirty Clothes, The	Sproul	RF		3	
Cleopatra	Stanley	B	I-2	1	
Yellow and Pink	Steig	Fa	TRA-1	1	
Dr. DeSoto	Steig	Fa		1	
Sylvester and the Magic Pebble	Steig	Fa		1	
Brave Irene	Steig	Fa		2	
Dominic	Steig	F		3	
Amos and Boris	Steig	Fa		1	
Child's Garden of Verses, A	Stevenson	P	M-2 TRA	3	
Daniel Boone	Stevenson	Fa	TRA-1	3	
Egyptians	Usborne	NF	I-2	1	
Time Train-Ancient Rome	Usborne	NF	I-3	2	
Who Built the Pyramids?	Usborne	NF	I-2	2	
18 Penny Goose, The	Walker	Fa		1	
Biggest Bear, The	Ward	F		2	
Boxcar Children, The (#1)	Warner	RF	M-2	2	
Boxcar Children sequels	Warner	RF		2	
Samuel Eaton's Day	Waters	HF		2	
Sarah Morton's Day	Waters	HF		2	
Charlotte's Web	White	Fa	M-3	3	
Stuart Little	White	Fa		3	
Trumpet of the Swan, The	White	Fa		3	
Little House in the Big Woods	Wilder	RF/HF	M-2	2	
Farmer Boy	Wilder	RF/HF		3	

Lower Grammar

Title	Author	Genre	Notations	Level	√
Little House on the Prairie (+ sequels)	Wilder	RF/HF		2	
Exodus	Wildsmith	H	I-2	1	
Joseph	Wildsmith	B	I-2	1	
Chair for My Mother, A	Williams	F		1	
Velveteen Rabbit	Williams	Fa	M-2 TRA	2	
Detectives in Togas	Winterfield	HF	I-3	3	
Christmas Miracle of Jonathan Toomey, The	Wojciechowski	RF		3	
Owl Moon	Yolen	RF		2	
New Coat for Anna, A	Ziefert	F		2	
Harry the Dirty Dog (+ any in series)	Zion	Fa		1	
Mr. Rabbit and the Lovely Present	Zolotow	Fa		1	
Big Sister and Little Sister	Zolotow	F		1	
Hold My Hand	Zolotow	F		1	
Storm Book, The	Zolotow	RF		1	

Additional Titles

Title	Author	Date read

notes:

notes:

notes:

notes:

notes:

notes:

notes:

notes:

notes:

notes:

notes:

Additional Titles

Title	Author	Date read

notes:

notes:

notes:

notes:

notes:

notes:

notes:

notes:

notes:

notes:

notes:

Additional Titles

Title	Author	Date read

notes:

notes:

notes:

notes:

notes:

notes:

notes:

notes:

notes:

notes:

notes:

Upper Grammar School List
(4ᵗʰ - 6ᵗʰ)

Title	Author	Genre	Notations	Level	√
Watership Down	Adams	Fa		3	
An Old Fashioned Girl	Alcott	RF		3	
Eight Cousins	Alcott	RF		3	
Little Men	Alcott	RF		3	
Little Women	Alcott	HF/RF	M-6	3	
Black Cauldron, The	Alexander	Fa		2	
Book of Three, The	Alexander	Fa		2	
Castle of Llyr	Alexander	Fa		2	
High King, The	Alexander	Fa		2	
Taran Wanderer	Alexander	Fa		2	
William Shakespeare and the Globe	Aliki	H	I-4	1	
Three Visitor's to Early Plymouth	Altham, Pory	H	I-5	1	
Cartier Sails the St. Lawrence	Averill	H	I-5	2	
Encounter at Easton	Avi	H	I-5	2	
Parallel Journeys	Ayer	H/B	I-6	3	
Coral Island, The	Ballantyne	Ad		2	
Eighteenth- Century Clothing at Williamsburg	Baumgarter	NF	I-5	1	
Theodore Roosevelt	Blackburn	B	TRA-6	3	
Gathering of Days, A	Blos	HF	I-6	3	
What's the Deal?	Blumberg	H	I-5	2	
Daniel Boone	Boone or Daugherty	B	I-5	2	

PAGE 26

Upper Grammar

Title	Author	Genre	Notations	Level	√
Stranded at Plimouth Plantation, 1626	Bowen	H	I-5	1	
Caddie Woodlawn	Brink	RF/H	I-6	3	
Homes in the Wilderness	Brown	H	I-5	2	
Sword in the Tree	Bulla	RF/H	I-4	1	
Viking Adventure	Bulla	RF/H	I-4	1	
John Billington	Bulla	B	I-5	1	
Little Lord Fauntleroy	Burnett	RF		2	
Little Princess	Burnett	RF		1	
Secret Garden	Burnett	RF		2	
Incredible Journey, The	Burnford	RF		2	
Oh, Pioneers!	Cather	H	I-6	3	
Soft Rain: A Story of the Cherokee Trail of Tears	Cornelissen	H/B	I-6	2	
Ben Franklin of Old Philadelphia	Cousins	B	I-5	1	
Boy in the Alamo, The	Cousins	HF	I-6	3	
Story of Thomas A. Edison	Cousins	B	I-6	2	
Davy Crockett: His Own Story	Crockett	AB	I-6	2	
Abraham Lincoln	D'Aulaire	B		1	
Columbus	D'Aulaire	B	I-5	1	
George Washington	D'Aulaire	B	I-5	1	
Pocahontas	D'Aulaire	B	I-5	1	
Landing of the Pilgrims	Daugherty	H	M-5	2	
Magna Charta	Daugherty	H	I-4	2	
Tale of Despereaux, The	DeCamillo	Fa		2	
Augustine, the Farmer's Boy of Tagaste	De Zeeuw	B	I-4	1	

Upper Grammar

Title	Author	Genre	Notations	Level	√
Carpenter of Zerbst	De Zeeuw	B	I-4	1	
Door in the Wall, The	DeAngeli	HF	TRA-4	1	
House of Sixty Fathers, The	DeJong	HF	I-6	2	
Christmas Carol, A	Dickens	Fa	M-6	3	
Hans Brinker or the Silver Skates	Dodge	RF		2	
King Arthur	Dover edition	Fa	M-4	1	
Alligator Case, The	Dubois	RF		1	
Twenty and Ten	Dubois	H	I-6	1	
Twenty-one Balloons	Dubois	F		1	
Journal of Otto Peltonen, The	Durbin	B/HF	I-6	3	
Matchlock Gun	Edmonds	HF	I-5	1	
Gone-away Lake	Enright	RF		2	
Return to Gone-away Lake	Enright	RF		2	
Thimble Summer	Enright	RF	I-6	2	
Ginger Pye	Estes	F		2	
Hundred Dresses, The	Estes	RF		1	
Moffats, The (+any sequels)	Estes	RF		1	
Pinky Pye	Estes	F		2	
Black Stallion, The	Farley	Ad		1	
Duel in the Wilderness	Farley	H	I-5	2	
Paul Revere and the Minutemen	Fisher	H	I-5	2	
Bull Run	Fleischman	HF	I-6	2	
Young Huguenots	Floyer	H	I-4	2	
Johnny Tremain	Forbes	HF	M-5	2	

Upper Grammar

Title	Author	Genre	Notations	Level	√
Diary of Anne Frank	Frank	AB	I-6	3	
Cowboys of the Wild West	Freedman	H	I-6	1	
Immigrant Kids	Freeman	H	I-6	1	
Story of Rolf and the Viking Bow	French	HF	TRA-4	3	
And Then What Happened, Paul Revere?	Fritz	H	I-5	1	
Brady	Fritz	HF	I-6	2	
Early Thunder	Fritz	HF	I-5	1	
Great Little Madison, The	Fritz	B	I-5	2	
Shh! We're Writing the Constitution	Fritz	H	I-5	1	
Stonewall Jackson	Fritz	B	I-6	1	
Traitor: The Case of Benedict Arnold	Fritz	B	I-5	2	
What's the Big Idea Ben Franklin?	Fritz	H	I-5	1	
Where Was Patrick Henry on the 29th of May?	Fritz	H	I-5	1	
Why Don't You Get a Horse, Sam Adams?	Fritz	H	I-5	1	
Why Not, Lafayette?	Fritz	H	I-5	1	
Will You Sign Here John Hancock?	Fritz	H	I-5	1	
Around the World in 100 Years	Fritz	H	I-5	3	
My Side of the Mountain	George	RF		1	
Lily's Crossing	Giff	H	I-6	2	
Old Yeller	Gipson	RF		2	
Memories of Anne Frank	Gold	NF	I-6	3	
Reluctant Dragon, The	Graham	Fa		1	

Upper Grammar

Title	Author	Genre	Notations	Level	√
Wind in the Willows	Graham	Fa		1	
Adam of the Road	Gray	HF	I-4	2	
Robin Hood	Green	Fa	M-4	2	
Cleopatra VII: Daughter of the Nile	Gregory	B		2	
Eleanor: Crown Jewel of Acquitaine	Gregory	B	I-4	2	
Book About Benjamin Franklin, A	Gross	B	I-5	2	
Jack Jouett's Ride	Haley	H	I-5	1	
Dangerous Journey	Hamori	H	I-6	3	
Amazing, Impossible Erie Canal	Harness	H	I-6	1	
They're Off! The Story of the Pony Express	Harness	H	I-6	1	
Three Young Pilgrims	Harness	H	I-5	1	
Young John Quincy	Harness	H	I-5	2	
Young John Quincy	Harness	B	I-5	1	
Battle of Gettysburg	Haskell	H	I-6	3	
Tanglewood Tales	Hawthorne	Fa		3	
Wonder Book	Hawthorne	Fa		3	
City in Winter, A	Helprin	Fa	TRA-6	3	
Justin Morgan Had a Horse	Henry	RF/H		1	
With Lee in Virginia	Henty	HF	I-6	3	
Hiroshima	Hershey	H	I-6	3	
Out of the Dust	Hesse	HF	I-6	2	
Timmy O'Dowd and the Big Ditch	Hilts	H	TRA-6	2	
Swamp Fox	Holbrook	B	I-5	2	

Upper Grammar

Title	Author	Genre	Notations	Level	√
North to Freedom	Holm	H	I-6	2	
Across Five Aprils	Hunt	HF	I-6	2	
Legends of Sleepy Hollow	Irving	Fa	TRA-5	2	
Rip Van Winkle	Irving	Fa		2	
Witchcraft of Salem Village	Jackson	H	I-5	2	
Trailblazer Books (series) (indiv. titles listed on history lit. list)	Jackson	B	I-5, 6	2	
Redwall	Jacques	Fa	TRA-4	1	
Redwall Series- any	Jacques	Fa		1	
Vikings, The	Janeway	H	I-4	2	
Little Colonel, The	Johnson	HF	I-6	2	
Dutch Color	Jones	HF		2	
Huguenot Garden	Jones	HF	M-4	2	
Scottish Seas	Jones	HF		2	
Benjamin Franklin	Judson	B	I-5	2	
Gettysburg	Kantor	H	M-6	2	
Rifles for Watie	Keith	H	I-6	2	
Surrender at Yorktown	Kent	H	I-5	2	
Just So Stories	Kipling	Fa		3	
Big Red	Kjelgaard	RF		1	
Journey to Monticello	Knight	H	I-5	1	
Winter at Valley Forge	Knight	H	I-5	1	
Jamestown: New World Adventure	Knight	H	I-5	1	
From the Mixed- up Files of Mrs. Basil E. Frankweiler	Konigsburg	RF		1	
Thirty Seconds Over Tokyo	Lawson	NF	I-6	3	
Swiftly Tilting Planet, A	L'Engle	Fa		2	

Upper Grammar

Title	Author	Genre	Notations	Level	√
Wind in the Door, A	L'Engle	Fa		2	
Wrinkle in Time	L'Engle	Fa	M-5	3	
Mary, Queen of Scots	Landmark Pub.	B	I-4	2	
Elizabeth I: Red Rose of the House of Tudor	Lasky	B	I-4	2	
Marie Antoinette: Princess of Versailles	Lasky	B	I-5	2	
Mary, Queen of Scots: Queen Without a Country	Lasky	B	I-4	2	
Anchors Aweigh: The Story of David Glasgow Farragut	Latham	B	I-5	2	
Carry on, Mr. Bowditch	Latham	B	I-5	2	
In the Hall of the Dragon King	Lawhead	Fa		3	
Sword and the Flame, The	Lawhead	Fa		3	
Warlords of Nin, The	Lawhead	Fa		3	
Thirty Seconds Over Tokyo	Lawson	H	I-6	2	
Almost Home	Lawton	HF	I-5	1	
Indian Captive	Lenski	HF	I-5	2	
If Your Name Was Changed at Ellis Island	Levine	H	I-6	1	
Journey to America	Levitin	HF	I-6	2	
Chronicles of Narnia- any	Lewis	Fa		1	
Lion, Witch & Wardrobe	Lewis	Fa	M-5	1	
Raoul Wallenberg	Linnea	H	I-6	3	
Paul Revere's Ride	Longfellow	H/P	I-5	1	
Number the Stars	Lowry	H	I-6	3	
Castle	Macaulay	NF	I-4	1	

Upper Grammar

Title	Author	Genre	Notations	Level	√
At the Back of the North Wind	MacDonald	Fa		3	
Golden Key, The	MacDonald	Fa		2	
Light Princess, The	MacDonald	Fa		1	
Princess and Curdie, The	MacDonald	Fa		1	
Princess and the Goblin, The	MacDonald	Fa		2	
Yanks are Coming, The	Marrin	HF	I-6	3	
Yankee Doodle Boy	Martin	HF	I-5	2	
Betsy Ross and the Flag	Mayer	H/B	I-5	2	
Iron Scouts of the Confederacy	McGiffin	HF	I-6	2	
Moccasin Trail	McGraw	HF	I-6	2	
Hey, Mac!	McMurdie	H/B	I-6	3	
Land of the Morning	McMurdie	AB	I-6	3	
California Gold Rush	McNeer	H	I-6	1	
Artist of the Reformation: Abrecht Durer	McPherson	B	I-4	1	
The River of Grace: The Story of John Calvin	McPherson	B	I-4	2	
Piece of Mountain, A	McPherson	B	I-4	2	
Ocean of Truth: the Story of Isaac Newton	McPherson	B	I-5	2	
Snow Treasure	McSwigan	HF	I-6	3	
Invincible Louisa	Meigs	B	I-6	3	
Isabel: Jewel of Castilla	Meyer	B	I-4-6	2	
Thomas Jefferson the Third President	Monsell	B	I-5	1	
Anne of Avonlea	Montgomery	RF		3	
Anne of Green Gables	Montgomery	RF		3	

Upper Grammar

Title	Author	Genre	Notations	Level	√
Overland in 1846: Diaries & Letters of the California – Oregon Trail	Morgan	H/B	I-6	2	
On to Oregon	Morrow	H	TRA-6	2	
Boys' War, The	Murphy	H	I-6	2	
Civil War Poetry, Anthology	Negri, ed.	H/P	I-6	3	
Railway Children, The	Nesbit	RF		2	
Abe Lincoln: Log Cabin to the White House	North	B	I-6	2	
George Washington, Frontier Colonel	North	B	I-5	2	
Borrowers, The	Norton	Fa		1	
Hawk That Dare Not Hunt by Day	O'Dell	B	I-4	2	
Island of the Blue Dolphins	O'Dell	RF		1	
Sarah Bishop	O'Dell	HF	I-5	2	
Streams to the River, River to the Sea	O'Dell	RF		3	
Tales From the Arabian Nights	Oxford Press	Fa		3	
Long Way From Chicago, A	Peck	RF	1-6	2	
Year Down Yonder, A	Peck	RF	1-6	2	
Life of Washington	Polland	B	I-5	2	
When the Morning Came (vol. 1)	Prins	HF	I-4	2	
Dispelling the Tyranny (vol. 2)	Prins	HF	I-4	2	
Lonely Sentinel, The (vol. 1)	Prins	HF	I-6	2	

Upper Grammar

Title	Author	Genre	Notations	Level	√
Hideout in the Swamp (vol. 2)	Prins	HF	I-6	2	
Grim Reaper, The (vol. 3)	Prins	HF	I-6	2	
Partisans, The (vol. 4)	Prins	HF	I-6	2	
Sabotage (vol. 5)	Prins	HF	I-6	2	
Otto of the Silver Hand	Pyle	HF	I-4	2	
Wonder Clock, The	Pyle	Fa		1	
It Began With a Parachute	Rang	HF	I-6	2	
Yearling, The	Rawlings	RF	M-6	3	
Summer of the Monkeys	Rawls	RF		2	
Where the Red Fern Grows	Rawls	RF	TRA-5	3	
Wright Brothers, The	Reynolds	H/B	I-6	2	
Story of Old Ironsides, The	Richards	H	I-5	1	
Light in the Forest	Richter	H	I-5	2	
Luther the Leader	Robinson	B	I-4	2	
I, Columbus. My Journal	Roop	AB	I-5	3	
Joan of Arc	Ross	B	I-4	2	
How We Crossed the West	Schanzer	H	I-5	1	
Dear America (series) (indiv. titles listed on history lit. list)	Scholastic	B	I-6	2	
Beowulf	Serraillier	Fa	M-4	3	
Black Beauty	Sewell	RF		3	
Killer Angels, The	Shaara	H	I-6	3	
Killer Angels Companion	Shaara	NF/H	I-6	3	
Alpha Centauri	Siegel	Fa		3	
Childhood of Famous Americans (indiv. titles listed on history lit. list)	Simon & Shuster	B	I-5, 6	2	

Upper Grammar

Title	Author	Genre	Notations	Level	√
Starry Messenger	Sis	B	I-4	1	
Minstrel in the Tower	Skurzynski	HF	I-4	1	
Bronze Bow, The	Speare	HF		2	
Calico Captive	Speare	HF	I-5	2	
Sign of the Beaver	Speare	RF	I-5	2	
Witch of Blackbird Pond	Speare	RF/HF	TRA-5	2	
Black Falcon	Sperry	HF	I-5	2	
Call it Courage	Sperry	Ad		2	
John Paul Jones: Fighting Sailor	Sperry	B	I-5	2	
Heidi	Spyri	RF		2	
Bard of Avon	Stanley	B	I-4	1	
Joan of Arc	Stanley	B	I-4	1	
Leonardo da Vinci	Stanley	B	I-4	1	
Charles Dickens, the Man Who had Great Expectations	Stanley/Vennema	B	I-6	1	
Buffalo Knife, The	Steele	HF	I-5	1	
Flaming Arrows	Steele	HF	I-5	1	
Lone Hunt, The	Steele	HF	I-5	1	
Perilous Road, The	Steele	HF	I-6	2	
Westward Adventure	Steele	B	I-6	3	
Declaration of Independence	Stein	NF	I-5	2	
Freedom Train	Sterling	HF	I-6	2	
Kidnapped	Stevenson	Ad/RF		3	
Treasure Island	Stevenson	Ad/RF	M-5	3	
Paul Revere	Stevenson	B	I-5	1	
Pioneers Go West	Stewart	H/B	I-6	1	
Alamo!	Sullivan	H	I-6	1	

Upper Grammar

Title	Author	Genre	Notations	Level	√
Lewis and Clark	Sullivan	H	I-5	2	
Balboa	Syme	B	I-5	3	
John Smith of Virginia	Syme	B	I-5	3	
Air Raid – Pearl Harbor	Taylor	H	I-6	3	
Roll of Thunder, Hear My Cry	Taylor	HF	I-6	3	
Hiding Place, The	Ten Boom	B	M-6	3	
Lad: A Dog	Terhune	RF		1	
Morning Star of the Reformation	Thomson	B	I-4	2	
Farmer Giles of Ham	Tolkien	Fa		3	
Fellowship of the Ring	Tolkien	Fa		3	
Hobbit, The	Tolkien	Fa	M-4	2	
Return of the King	Tolkien	Fa		3	
Two Towers, The	Tolkien	Fa		3	
Story of the Trapp Family Singers	Trapp	B	I-6	3	
Shadow of the Hawk	Trease	HF		2	
Adventures of Huckleberry Finn	Twain	RF		3	
Adventures of Tom Sawyer	Twain	RF		3	
Prince and the Pauper, The	Twain	RF		3	
Tom Sawyer Abroad	Twain	Ad		2	
Tom Sawyer Detective	Twain	Ad		2	
Knights	Usborne	NF	I-4	1	
Viking World	Usborne	NF	I-4	3	
What Where Castles For?	Usborne	NF	I-4	1	
William of Orange	Van de Hulst	B	I-4	2	

Upper Grammar

Title	Author	Genre	Notations	Level	√
Escape, The	Van der Jagt	Ad	I-4	2	
Secret Mission, The	Van der Jagt	Ad	I-4	2	
Three Men Came to Heidelberg	Van Halsema	H	I-4	2	
Around the World in Eighty Days	Verne	Fa		3	
From the Earth to the Moon	Verne	Fa		3	
Journey to the Center of the Earth	Verne	Fa		3	
Beggar's Bible, The	Vernon	B	I-4	2	
Heart Strangely Warmed, A	Vernon	B	I-5	2	
Ink on His Fingers	Vernon	HF	I-4	1	
Man Who Laid the Egg, The	Vernon	B	I-4	2	
Thunderstorm in the Church	Vernon	HF	I-4	1	
Strangers in the Land	Vernon	HF	I-4	2	
Co. Aytch	Watkins	H	I-6	3	
We Were There with Richard the Lionhearted and the Third Crusade	Webb	HF	TRA-4	1	
Saint Francis	Wildsmith	B	I-4	1	
If All the Swords in England: A Story of Thomas Becket	Willard	B	I-4	2	
John Paul Jones	Worcester	B	I-5	2	
Guns for General Washington	Wright	HF	I-5	2	
Swiss Family Robinson	Wyss	RF/HF		3	

Upper Grammar

Title	Author	Genre	Notations	Level	√
Amos Fortune, Free Man	Yates	HF	I-6	2	
Sergeant York	York	AB/H	M-6	2	
Nathan Hale, Patriot Spy	Zemlicka	B	I-5	2	

Additional Titles

Title	Author	Date read

notes:

notes:

notes:

notes:

notes:

notes:

notes:

notes:

notes:

notes:

notes:

Additional Titles

Title	Author	Date read

notes:

notes:

notes:

notes:

notes:

notes:

notes:

notes:

notes:

notes:

notes:

Additional Titles

Title	Author	Date read

notes:

notes:

notes:

notes:

notes:

notes:

notes:

notes:

notes:

notes:

notes:

Dialectic School List
(7th - 9th)

Title	Author	Genre	Notations	Level	√
Eight Cousins	Alcott	RF		2	
Jack and Jill	Alcott	RF		1	
Jo's Boys	Alcott	RF		1	
Little Men	Alcott	RF		1	
King's Shadow, The	Alder	HF	I-9	1	
Story of A Bad Boy	Aldrich	AB		1	
Iron Ring, The	Alexander	HF	M-7	1	
Meditations	Aurelius			3	
Here I Stand: A Life of Martin Luther	Bainton	B	I-9	3	
Life of John Calvin, The	Beza	B	I-9	3	
Good Earth, The	Buck	H	M-7	1	
Last Days of Pompeii	Bulwer-Lytton	H	I-8	3	
Last of the Barons	Bulwer-Lytton	H	I-9	3	
Reinzi, the Last of the Roman Tribunes	Bulwer-Lytton	H	I-9	3	
Summer of the Swans	Byars	F		1	
Canterbury Tales	Chaucer (Norton)	Fa	I-9	3	
Father Brown Stories	Chesterton	M		2	
St. Francis of Assisi	Chesterton	B	I-9	3	
St. Thomas Aquinas: The Dumb Ox	Chesterton	B	I-9	3	
Selections	Copernicus	NF	I-9	3	
Robinson Crusoe	DeFoe	RF/Ad		2	

PAGE 43

Dialectic

Title	Author	Genre	Notations	Level	√
David Copperfield	Dickens	RF		3	
Oliver Twist	Dickens	RF		3	
Hound of the Baskervilles	Doyle	M		1	
Adventures of Sherlock Holmes, The	Doyle	M		1	
Count of Monte-Cristo	Dumas	RF/Ad		3	
Three Musketeers	Dumas	RF/Ad		3	
Murder in the Cathedral	Eliot	P/B	I-9	3	
Horatio Hornblower Series	Forester	RF/Ad		3	
Story of Rolf and the Viking Bow	French	HF		1	
Lost Baron, The	French	HF	I-9	2	
Red Keep, The	French	HF	I-9	2	
Tales of Ancient Egypt	Green	HF	I-7	1	
Beric the Briton	Henty	HF	I-8	2	
Cat of Bubastes, The	Henty	HF	I-7	1	
Dragon and the Raven	Henty	HF	I-9	2	
Henty Historical Series	Henty	HF		2	
St. Bartholomew's Eve	Henty	HF	I-9	2	
Young Carthaginian	Henty	HF	I-8	1	
St. George for England	Henty	HF	I-9	2	
In Freedom's Cause	Henty	HF	I-9	2	
Iliad, The	Homer	P/Fa/H	M-8	2	
Odyssey, The	Homer	P/Fa/H	I-8	3	
Hunchback of Notre Dame	Hugo	RF	I-9	3	
Hinds' Feet on High Places	Hurnard	Fa		2	
Legend of Sleepy Hollow	Irving	Fa		1	

Dialectic

Title	Author	Genre	Notations	Level	√
Rip Van Winkle	Irving	Fa		1	
Hidden Treasure of Glaston	Jewett	HF	I-9	2	
Captains Courageous	Kipling	Ad/RF		1	
Jungle Book, The	Kipling	Fa		1	
Kim	Kipling	HF		2	
Unaborted Socrates, The	Kreeft	F		3	
Best Things in Life, The	Kreeft	F		3	
Aeschylus I	Lattimore	H/D	I-8	3	
Dragon King Trilogy	Lawhead	Fa		2	
Pendragon Cycle Trilogy	Lawhead	Fa		2	
Escape from Egypt	Levitin	HF	I-7	1	
Chronicles of Narnia	Lewis	Fa		1	
Till We Have Faces	Lewis	Fa	I-8	3	
At the Back of the North Wind	MacDonald	Fa		1	
Sir Gibbie	MacDonald	RF		2	
Prince, The	Machiavelli (Norton)	H	I-9	3	
Golden Goblet, The	McGraw	HF	I-7	1	
Mara, Daughter of the Nile	McGraw	HF	I-7	1	
Coronation of Glory: The Story of Lady Jane Gray	Meroft	B	I-9	1	
Utopia	More	F	I-9	3	
Road To Damietta	O' Dell	RF	I-9	2	
Black Pearl, The	O'Dell	RF		2	
Kings Fifth, The	O'Dell	RF/HF		2	
Animal Farm	Orwell	Fa		1	

Dialectic

Title	Author	Genre	Notations	Level	√
Bridge to Terabithia	Paterson	RF		2	
Pharaohs of Ancient Egypt	Payne	H	I-7	1	
Epic of Gilgamesh	Penguin	H/P	M-7	2	
Chronicles of Brother Cadfael	Peters	M	I-9	3	
Last Days of Socrates	Plato	H	I-8	3	
Scottish Chiefs	Porter	HF	I-9	2	
Book of Pirates	Pyle	Ad		1	
Men of Iron	Pyle	HF/Ad		1	
Otto of the Silver Hand	Pyle	HF		1	
Oxford Book of English Verse	Quiller-Couch	P		3	
Swallows and Amazons	Ransome	Ad/RF		1	
Ides of April, The	Ray	HF	I-8	1	
Beyond the Desert Gate	Ray	HF	I-8	1	
Beowulf	Rebsamen	P/H	M-9	3	
Nine Tailors, The	Sayers	M		3	
Abbott, The	Scott	HF	I-9	3	
Ivanhoe	Scott	HF	M-9	3	
Lady of the Lake	Scott	HF	I-9	3	
Quentin Durward	Scott	HF	I-9	2	
Talisman, The	Scott	HF	I-9	3	
Macbeth	Shakespeare	D	M-9	3	
Julius Caesar	Shakespeare	D	M-8	3	
Five Little Peppers and How They Grew	Sidney	RF		1	
Quo Vadis	Sienkiewicz	HF	M-8	2	
Theras & His Town	Snedeker	HF	I-8	1	
Black Falcon	Sperry	Ad		1	

Dialectic

Title	Author	Genre	Notations	Level	√
Twice Freed	St. John	HF	I-8	1	
Red Pony, The	Steinbeck	RF		1	
Black Arrow, The	Stevenson	RF/HF	I-9	1	
Kidnapped	Stevenson	Ad/RF		2	
Treasure Island	Stevenson	Ad/RF		1	
Black Ships Before Troy	Sutcliff	HF	I-8	2	
Blood Feud	Sutcliff	HF		3	
Eagle of the Ninth	Sutcliff	HF	I-8	2	
Lantern Bearers, The	Sutcliff	HF	I-9	2	
Outcast, The	Sutcliff	HF	I-8	2	
Silver Branch, The	Sutcliff	HF	I-8	2	
Wanderings of Odysseus	Sutcliff	Fa	I-8	2	
Sword Song	Sutcliff	RF		3	
Shining Company, The	Sutcliff	HF	I-9	2	
Idylls of the King	Tennyson	P/Fa	I-9	3	
Lord of the Rings Trilogy	Tolkien	Fa		1	
Sir Gawain and the Green Knight	Tolkien	Fa	I-9	2	
Tirzah	Travis	HF	I-7	1	
Escape to King Alfred	Trease	HF		1	
Adventures of Huckleberry Finn	Twain	RF	M-7	1	
Adventures of Tom Sawyer	Twain	RF		1	
Connecticut Yankee in King Arthur's Ct.	Twain	RF		2	
Joan of Arc	Twain	B	I-9	2	
Life on the Mississippi	Twain	RF		2	
Prince and the Pauper	Twain	RF		1	
This Was John Calvin	Van Halsema	B	I-9	1	

Dialectic

Title	Author	Genre	Notations	Level	√
Robin Hood	various	Fa	I-9	1	
Tales of King Arthur	various	Fa	I-9	1	
Mysterious Island, The	Verne	Fa		1	
Twenty Thous. Leagues Under the Sea	Verne	Fa		1	
Ben Hur	Wallace	HF	I-8	2	
Invisible Man, The	Wells	SF		1	
Time Machine, The	Wells	SF		1	
War of the Worlds	Wells	SF		1	
Rebecca of Sunnybrook Farm	Wiggen	RF		1	
Augustine Came to Kent	Willard	HF		2	
Lark and the Laurel, The	Willard	HF		2	
Son of Charlemagne	Willard	HF		2	
God King	Williamson	H	I-7	1	
Swiss Family Robinson	Wyss	RF		1	

Additional Titles

Title	Author	Date read

notes:

notes:

notes:

notes:

notes:

notes:

notes:

notes:

notes:

notes:

notes:

Additional Titles

Title	Author	Date read

notes:

notes:

notes:

notes:

notes:

notes:

notes:

notes:

notes:

notes:

notes:

Additional Titles

Title	Author	Date read

notes:

notes:

notes:

notes:

notes:

notes:

notes:

notes:

notes:

notes:

notes:

Rhetoric School List
(10th - 12th)

Title	Author	Genre	Notations	Level	√
Confessions	Augustine	AB		2	
Emma	Austen	RF		1	
Pride and Prejudice	Austen	RF	M-10	1	
Sense and Sensibility	Austen	RF		1	
Here I Stand: A Life of Martin Luther	Bainton	B		1	
Journals of Lewis and Clark	Bakeless	H/B	I-11	1	
Waiting for Godot	Beckett	D	M-12	3	
Lorna Doone	Blackmore	RF/HF		3	
Fahrenheit 451	Bradbury	SF		2	
Martian Chronicles	Bradbury	SF		2	
Of Plymouth Plantation	Bradford	AB	I-11	3	
Jane Eyre	Bronte	RF	M-10	1	
Villette	Bronte	RF		2	
Wuthering Heights	Bronte	RF		2	
God's Smuggler	Brother Andrew	B		2	
Greenmantle	Buchan	Ad		1	
Thirty-Nine Steps	Buchan	Ad		1	
Pilgrim's Progress	Bunyan	Fa	M-10	1	
Alice in Wonderland	Carroll	Fa		1	
Death Comes for the Archbishop	Cather	RF		3	
My Antonia	Cather	RF/HF	I-11	2	
Don Quixote de la Mancha (abridged)	Cervantes	F		1	
Witness	Chambers			2	

Rhetoric

Title	Author	Genre	Notations	Level	√
Canterbury Tales	Chaucer	P		3	
A Man Called Thursday	Chesterton	F		2	
Everlasting Man	Chesterton	NF		2	
Rime of the Ancient Mariner, The	Coleridge	P		1	
Heart of Darkness	Conrad	RF	M-10	2	
Lord Jim	Conrad	RF		2	
Last of the Mohicans	Cooper	HF	M-11	2	
Silver Chalice, The	Costain	HF/RF		1	
Red Badge of Courage	Crane	HF	I-11	2	
Divine Comedy	Dante	P		2	
David Copperfield	Dickens	RF		3	
Great Expectations	Dickens	RF	M-10	1	
Hard Times	Dickens	RF		3	
Oliver Twist	Dickens	RF		1	
Pickwick Papers	Dickens	RF		3	
Tale of Two Cities, A	Dickens	RF/HF	I-12	1	
Brothers Karamazov	Dostoyevsky	RF		4	
Crime and Punishment	Dostoyevsky	RF		4	
Grand Inquisitor, The	Dostoyevsky	RF	M-12	3	
Notes from Underground	Dostoevsky	RF		2	
Magnificent Obsession	Douglas	RF		1	
Robe, The	Douglas	HF		1	
Count of Monte Cristo	Dumas	RF/AD		1	
Rebecca	DuMaurier	RF		1	
Name of the Rose, The	Ecco	HF	I-12	3	
Adam Bede	Eliot	RF		3	
Middlemarch	Eliot	RF		3	
Mill on the Floss	Eliot	RF		2	

Rhetoric

Title	Author	Genre	Notations	Level	√
Silas Marner	Eliot	RF	M-10	1	
Through Gates of Splender (Jim Elliot)	Elliot	B		1	
Essays	Emerson	P		2	
Peace Like a River	Enger	RF		1	
Great Gatsby, The	Fitzgerald	RF	M-11	2	
Horatio Hornblower Series	Forester	Ad		1	
Foxe's Book of Martyrs	Foxe (Berry, ed.)	B		1	
Autobiography	Franklin	AB	I-11	2	
Sophie's World	Gaardner	F		2	
Jonathan & Sarah: An Uncommon Union	Gerstner	B	I-11	2	
Idelette: The Life of Mrs. John Calvin	Gerstner	B		2	
Not A Tame Lion (C.S. Lewis)	Glaspey	B		2	
Faust	Goethe	F		3	
Lord of the Flies	Golding	RF		2	
House of Seven Gables	Hawthorne	RF		2	
Scarlett Letter, The	Hawthorne	RF	M-11	2	
Mourt's Relation: A Journal of the Pilgrims at Plymouth	Heath	B	I-11	2	
A Farewell to Arms	Hemingway	RF		3	
All Creatures Great and Small	Herriot	RF		1	
Hunchback of Notre Dame	Hugo	F		1	
Les Miserables (abridged-James Robinson)	Hugo	RF/HF	I-12	2	
Les Miserables (unabridged)	Hugo	RF/HF	I-12	3-4	
American, The	James	RF	M-12	3	
Brave New World	Huxley	RF	M-12	3	

PAGE 54

Rhetoric

Title	Author	Genre	Notations	Level	√
Portrait of A Lady	James	RF		3	
Turn of the Screw	James	F		3	
What's with the Mutant in the Microscope?	Johnson & White	NF		1	
Portrait of the Artist as a Young Man, A	Joyce		M-12	3	
All Quiet on the Western Front	Remarque	HF		3	
To Kill a Mockingbird	Lee	RF/HF		2	
Mere Christianity	Lewis	NF		3	
Out of the Silent Planet	Lewis	SF	M-10	1	
Perelandra	Lewis	SF		1	
That Hideous Strength	Lewis	SF		2	
Pilgrim's Regress	Lewis	Fa		3	
Screwtape Letters	Lewis	Fa		1	
Great Divorce, The	Lewis	Fa		2	
Call of the Wild	London	Ad		2	
Sea Wolf, The	London	Ad		1	
White Fang	London	Ad		1	
Bondage of the Will, The	Luther	NF		2	
Never Give In (Winston Churchill)	Mansfield	B		2	
Forgotten Founding Father: Whitefield	Mansfield	B	I-11	2	
Doctor Faustus	Marlowe	F		3	
Communist Manifesto	Marx	NF		3	
Moby Dick	Melville	Ad/RF	M-11	3	
Death of a Salesman	Miller	D	M-12	2	
Paradise Lost	Milton	P	M-10	2	

Rhetoric

Title	Author	Genre	Notations	Level	√
Gone With the Wind	Mitchell	RF/HF	I-11	2	
Utopia	More	F		2	
Jonathan Edwards: A New Biography	Murray	B	I-11	3	
Norton Anthology of American Literature (shorter 6th edition – selections)	Norton	F	M-11	2	
A Good Man is Hard to Find	O'Connor	RF		2	
Everything That Rises Must Converge	O'Connor	RF		3	
Scarlet Pimpernel	Orczy	Ad/HF	I-12	1	
1984	Orwell	F	M-12	2	
Oregon Trail	Parkman	HF	I-11	2	
Dr. Zhivago	Pasternak	HF	I-12	3	
Cry of the Beloved Country	Paten	H	M-12	3	
Amusing Ourselves to Death	Postman	NF		3	
Stepping Heavenward	Prentiss	B		1	
Twentieth Maine, The	Pullen	HF	I-11	2	
Oxford Book of English Verse- selections	Quiller-Couch	P		1	
Northwest Passage	Roberts	HF	I-11	2	
Worldly Saints	Ryken	H	I-11	3	
Lord Peter and other mysteries	Sayers	M		1	
God's and Generals	Shaara	H	I-11	1	
Killer Angels, The	Shaara	H	I-11	1	
Rise to Rebellion	Shaara	H	I-11	1	
This Glorious Cause	Shaara	H	I-11	1	

Rhetoric

Title	Author	Genre	Notations	Level	√
As You Like It	Shakespeare	D	M-12	1	
Hamlet	Shakespeare	D	M-10	1	
King Lear	Shakespeare	D		2	
Merchants of Venice, The	Shakespeare	D		1	
Midsummer Night's Dream, A	Shakespeare	D		1	
Romeo and Juliet	Shakespeare	D		1	
Shakespeare- any works	Shakespeare	D		1-3	
Richard III	Shakespeare	D	I-12	3	
Henry V	Shakespeare	D	I-10	3	
Much Ado About Nothing	Shakespeare	D		2	
Frankenstein	Shelley	F	M-12	1	
Through the Shadowlands: The Story of his Life with Joy Davidman (C.S. Lewis)	Sibley	B		1	
Jungle, The	Sinclair	F	M-11	2	
One Day in the Life of Ivan Denisovich	Solzhenitsyn	RF/HF	M-12	3	
Sophocles I	Sophocles	D		3	
Oedipus Rex	Sophocles	D	M-12	3	
Grapes of Wrath	Steinbeck	RF/HF	I-11	2	
Pearl, The	Steinbeck	RF		1	
Dr. Jekyll & Mr. Hyde	Stevenson	RF	M-12	1	
Uncle Tom's Cabin	Stowe	RF/HF	M-11	2	
Gulliver's Travels	Swift	HF	M-10	2	
Idylls of the King	Tennyson	P	I-10	2	
Daughter of Time, The	Tey	M	I-10	1	
Vanity Fair	Thackeray	F		3	
Walden	Thoreau	NF		2	

Rhetoric

Title	Author	Genre	Notations	Level	√
Anna Karenina	Tolstoy	HF	I-12	3	
War and Peace	Tolstoy	HF	I-12	4	
Fathers and Sons	Turgenev	RF		4	
Severe Mercy, A	Vanauken	AB		3	
Give Me Liberty: The Uncompromising Statesmanship of Patrick Henry	Vaughn	B	I-11	2	
Postmodern Times	Veith	NF		3	
Aeneid, The	Virgil	P/H	I-12	3	
Candide	Voltaire	RF/HF		3	
Up From Slavery	Washington	B	I-11	2	
Ethan Frome	Wharton	RF		2	
Picture of Dorian Gray	Wilde	F		3	
Importance of Being Earnest, The	Wilde	D		2	
Call of Duty (Robert E. Lee)	Wilkins	B	I-11	1	
Glass Menagerie, The	Williams	D		2	
For Kirk & Covenant (John Knox)	Wilson	B		2	
Beyond Stateliest Marble: The Passionate Femininity of Anne Bradstreet	Wilson	B	I-11	2	
Leave it to Psmith	Wodehouse	RF		1	
Very Good, Jeeves	Wodehouse	RF		1	

Additional Titles

Title	Author	Date read

notes:

notes:

notes:

notes:

notes:

notes:

notes:

notes:

notes:

notes:

notes:

Additional Titles

Title	Author	Date read

notes:

notes:

notes:

notes:

notes:

notes:

notes:

notes:

notes:

notes:

notes:

Additional Titles

Title	Author	Date read

notes:

notes:

notes:

notes:

notes:

notes:

notes:

notes:

notes:

notes:

notes:

Additional Titles

Title	Author	Date read

notes:

notes:

notes:

notes:

notes:

notes:

notes:

notes:

notes:

notes:

notes:

Additional Titles

Title	Author	Date read

notes:

notes:

notes:

notes:

notes:

notes:

notes:

notes:

notes:

notes:

notes:

Additional Titles

Title	Author	Date read

notes:

notes:

notes:

notes:

notes:

notes:

notes:

notes:

notes:

notes:

notes:

Additional Titles

Title	Author	Date read

notes:

notes:

notes:

notes:

notes:

notes:

notes:

notes:

notes:

notes:

notes:

Additional Titles

Title	Author	Date read

notes:

notes:

notes:

notes:

notes:

notes:

notes:

notes:

notes:

notes:

notes:

Additional Titles

Title	Author	Date read

notes:

notes:

notes:

notes:

notes:

notes:

notes:

notes:

notes:

notes:

notes:

Additional Titles

Title	Author	Date read

notes:

notes:

notes:

notes:

notes:

notes:

notes:

notes:

notes:

notes:

notes:

the art of
POETRY

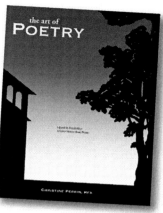

If you have ever felt mystified by, or unable to enjoy the significance of poetry, this book will lead you step-by-step to understanding and love of this branch of literature, guided by a gifted poet and teacher. *The Art of Poetry* is an excellent middle school or high school curriculum; it teaches the practice of reading a poem slowly and carefully, and introduces students to the elements of poetry (such as imagery and metaphor) and the many forms that can make a poem, from sonnet to open verse. In the belief that practice is the best way to learn, this book is rich with explications, exercises, and activities. A biography of each poet is also included, along with a CD of a reading of many of the poems.

Find samples and more information at www.ClassicalAcademicPress.com.

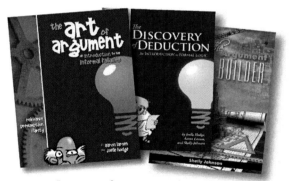

"My chief objection to a quarrel," Chesterton wrote, "is that it ends a *good argument.*"

Logic is a fascinating subject for students in middle school or high school. As a fundamental part of the trivium, logic study will impart to students the skills needed to craft accurate statements and identify the flawed arguments found so frequently in editorials, commercials, newspapers, journals and every other media. We regard the mastery of logic as a "paradigm" subject by which we evaluate, assess and learn other subjects—it is a sharp knife with which we can carve and shape all manner of wood. Mastery of logic is a requisite skill for mastering other subjects.

There are several branches of logic, and our three levels of curriculum focus on teaching informal and formal logic, as well as supplying students with the tools to create their own logical arguments. The three texts are modular, and while we generally recommend that students begin with informal logic study in *The Art of Argument*, the following two texts, *Discovery of Deduction* and *The Argument Builder*, can be used in any order. Each of these logic courses recognize that students are living in the 21st century and couch the logical concepts in real-life, often humorous examples.

Find samples and more information at www.ClassicalAcademicPress.com.

Latin is a rich, ancient language, and is still very much alive in the languages that we speak today. It plays a vital role in a classical education, training students in grammar, how a language works, and how to think critically. Learning Latin greatly expands English vocabulary and introduces students to the original work of some of the most influential writers in history.

Caveat emptor (let the buyer beware), these programs have made Latin the favorite subject of many students around the nation!

Song School Latin
A delightful introduction to Latin, designed for the youngest of students. *Song School Latin* is full of songs, stories, and activities. An album of 30 catchy songs on an audio CD is included with the program. Kindergarten through 3rd Grade.

Latin for Children
Our classic grammar school Latin program. Solid, clearly taught, engaging, and effective, LFC is a three year program including DVDs and Chant CDs, Activity Books, and History Readers and more! Don't forget all of the LFC Freebies! 3rd grade and up.

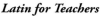

Latin Alive!
Learn how Latin still affects so many aspects of our culture today. Latin Alive! is full of translation and reading, Roman history and mythology. It is both an introduction for the upper school student who has not yet studied the language, and an excellent, deeper, continuation of grammar school study. 7th grade and up.

Latin for Teachers
Over 16 hours of professional Latin training for new and intermediate Latin teachers in schools or homeschools. Karen Moore, author of the new Latin Alive, the Latin for Children History Readers, and accomplished teacher herself, gives a bird's-eye view of the Latin language for teachers and adults.

Find samples and more information at www.ClassicalAcademicPress.com.